INDUSTRIAL RAILWAYS in COLOUR SOUTH

Copyright Irwell Press,
ISBN-978-1-906919-39-9
First published in 2011 by Irwell Press Ltd., 59A, High Street, Clophill, Bedfordshire, MK45 4BE
Printed by Konway Press.

With the passing of the years it is difficult to recall when my fascination with industrial railways was born. Flicking through tired notebooks suggested my first visit was to East Greenwich Gas Works in April 1957. That visit opened up a new world to explore and the hunt was on to track down these characterful systems with a diverse range of steam locomotives from the highly polished to those with liberal coatings of grime. Information on their whereabouts was not always easy to find but membership of the Railway Enthusiasts Club and the Birmingham Locomotive Club-Industrial Locomotive Information Section fuelled the explorations. Other locations rapidly followed in the same year. The enchantment of visits to the Millwall and Royal Docks, Dagenham Dock, Beckton and Purfleet spread to Barrington and Wissington, the ironstone country of the East Midlands and the Lancashire Coalfield. In the ensuing years most corners of the United Kingdom were covered. It was in 1960 that I switched from black and white film to colour. However I later returned to pursue the craft of using black and white alongside colour film.

London has a particular appeal as my city of birth. In the sixties the capital was still affectionately known as 'The Smoke' and with good reason. Amidst the close knit housing of East London; gas works, power stations, chemical and tanning works still gave freely of their toxic vapours. Most of the industry was concentrated along the Thames which still provided an economic means of transport despite the advent of railways. Confluent with the Thames are the Medway and the Lea whose banks were also home to heavy industry. Taking the Docklands Light Railway through a panorama of familiar names like Custom House and Gallions Reach it was hard to recognize remnants of the past. The dismal marshes at Beckton were a reminder that this terrain was originally purchased for the sprawl of Beckton Gas Works. Nowadays with the countrywide shrinkage of sites boasting industrial locomotives there is only a sprinkling to be found in Greater London.

Nevertheless, on a visit to Ford's of Dagenham in August, 2009 it was heartening to enjoy their diesel locomotives still bedecked with the Ford logo and royal blue livery reminiscent of steam days.

The focus of the book is on the old County of London and the Home Counties with an excursion into Hampshire and a cross border visit into Cambridgeshire from Hertfordshire. Thanks are due to life-long friend Anthony Janes (who accompanied me on forays in the sixties) for his encouragement as well as his wife, Glenys, for assisting with amendments to the text. Bob Darvill and Robin Waywell of the Industrial Railway Society have been invaluable in providing historical information from their archives. My 'art buddy' Sundar Walker has continued to support me in my publishing ventures.

Michael Poulter, Grange-Over-Sands, Cumbria

Several main line locomotives were fortunate enough to enjoy an after life in industrial service. This was particularly true of the ex-LSWR B4 class. Their short wheelbase made them eminently suitable for the tight curves which were often found in industrial yards. 30096 was sold to Corrall Limited in December 1963 for use at their coal wharf on the west bank of the River Itchen in Southhampton. Their sidings connected with the Southern Region Main Line near Northam Station. Here there was more good fortune for on a visit on the 20th August 1966 the B4 was found to be in the care of an ex-British Railways Driver from Southampton Docks. However the arrival of a Baguley diesel fom Bass at Burton-on-Trent in February, 1968 brought about the demise of steam working.

A familiar sight from trains on the Midland Main Line from St.Pancras was the towering chimneys of Coronation Brickworks situated at Kempston Hardwick in Marston Vale south of Bedford. It was opened in 1935 and acquired by the London Brick Company in 1936. Apart from a narrow gauge cable hauled system that served the extensive open pit exploiting sub surface clay, the works was also provided with standard gauge sidings. These connected with the down side of the main line at Houghton Conquest signal box terminating in the loading platforms at the kilns. This system was electrified and was unusual in being fitted with a 'trolleybus' style twin wire overhead. RUTH (English Electric:W/No.899 of 1935) had these tracks all to herself until scrapping in January 1971. During that time she sported various liveries. When delivered new to the site RUTH was bedecked in light green which later became yellow. On the 29th September 1962 her final colour of dull red was photographed. The works closed in 1974 and in 1980 was demolished, felling no less than eighteen chimneys.

The Home Counties of Bedfordshire and Buckinghamshire ring the London Basin with the chalk escarpment of the Chiltern Hills and chalky grasslands. So it comes as no surprise that the cement and lime industries hoved in to quarry this bounty. The cement works at Houghton Regis, lying just outside the north east environs of Dunstable, was built in the twenties. It was situated to the north of the ex-GNR Dunstable-Luton branch, east of Dunstable North station, with which it formed a triangular junction. On the 29th September,1962 there was an eclectic mixture of traction at the works. Here PUNCH HULL (Andrew Barclay:W/No.776 of 1896, rebuilt Baker 1928) takes a break. Resting in the shed was TOM PARRY (Andrew Barclay: W/No.2015 of 1935). The mortal remains of two aged John Fowler diesel locomotives (SEWELL W/No.21322 of 1936 and 7144 HOUGHTON W/No. 21941 of 1937) were decaying in the yard. The story was that a few weeks before, GRAHAMS, another John Fowler diesel withdrawn in 1959, (W/No.21455 of 1936) had departed for BPCM Penarth and had been reconstituted as one 'good' loco. from all three.

Industrial railways enthusiasts visiting the cement works at Dunstable (Houghton Regis) were delighted to find that not only did the works have a railway system but another self contained rail system existed to serve a large chalk quarry. This was to be found on the opposite side of the A5120 road to the works. On the 29th September 1962 this ancient locomotive (Motor Rail:W/No.3786 of 1925) was at work on equally ancient looking wagons loaded with overburden. At one time petrol mechanical but undergoing a life change to diesel mechanical this machine had been destined for a more distinguished career. It was originally ordered by the GWR in April 1923 as Motor Rail 2215 but was never delivered. On the same day Ruston and Hornsby diesel 425477 of 1959 was also at work whilst Ruston and Hornsby diesel 421437 of 1958 was under repair. In March 1971 cement manufacture ceased and the works became a distribution depot. Meanwhile back in 1965 the Luton to Dunstable branch had been closed to passengers with a section from Luton retained for industrial rail sidings. Rail traffic ceased in June 1988 when Ruston and Hornsby 425477 was the only locomotive left on site. The depot closed the following month. The last remnants of the branch closed to all traffic in 1990.

Two miles from Dunstable North Station just east of Stanbridgeford Station on the Leighton Buzzard Branch, the chalk extraction industry had another base. A trailing connection entered the Totternhoe works and quarries of the Rugby Portland Cement Company. In the 1930's it had acquired most of the chalk quarrying of the Totternhoe Lime and Stone Company. The rail system was unusual in that the exchange sidings were connected to the quarries by a cable worked incline. One locomotive worked the exchange sidings from its solitary engine shed whilst the quarry engine shed held up to four locomotives, all of which could be in use when the quarry was working to full capacity. Modernisation of the locomotive fleet in the fifties and sixties saw the arrival of five standard 100hp Sentinels of which two were delivered new. All were in green livery with yellow and green striped ends although Sentinel 9564 of 1954 photographed outside the quarry shed on 29th September 1962 had escaped this treatment. Subsequent quarrying developments were terminated in 1965 when the company began piping chalk slurry from its Kensworth Quarry (near Whipsnade) to Southam and Rugby replacing the rail traffic from Totternhoe. All five sentinels plus the Avonside found new homes in industry.

Moving south to the western suburbs of the Metropolis, the old County of London was home to Kensal Green Gas Works. A short walk along the Grand Junction Canal from Old Oak Lane took enthusiasts clutching tatty notebooks through a hole in the wall into the smoky interior of the Old Oak Common Locomotive Sheds. Few would have meandered a further mile along the canal to be in sight of Kensal Green Gas Works. Built on the inside of a large curve in the canal, gas production began here in 1845. In 1872 the plant was absorbed by the tentacles of the Gas Light and Coke Company. From 1851 coal was delivered by barge into a dock within gas works property. Rail connection was afforded to the internal system from the ex-Great Western Main Lines about two miles west of Paddington Station. On the 14th April 1962 KG No.6 was the sole steam locomotive (Bagnall:W/No.2172 of 1921) and that was out of use. Only two months later KG No.6 had been scrapped. Two diminutive diesels, built by Ruston and Hornsby in 1938 and Hibberd in 1951, were on hand to share the work. Rail traffic finished in March 1970 with the end of gas manufacture here.

Only a half a mile westwards along the towpath of the Grand Junction Canal from Old Oak Lane was the bulk of Acton Lane Generating Station. Such a walk would have crossed the boundary from the County of London into the erstwhile Middlesex. The plant was bounded by a triangle.To the south was the Grand Junction Canal, to the west Acton Lane and to the east the Cross-London Line of the ex-Midland Railway. The northern apex of the triangle was sliced by the ex-London and North Western Main Line from Euston. It was this latter route that connected with the internal sidings. The smoke pall from the sprawl of Willesden Locomotive Sheds would have drifted across the site but the embankment carrying the Cross-London line ensured that the locomotives were blocked from view. As for the power station's locomotives, only two were on offer on the 14th April 1962. ERGON (Robert Stephenson and Hawthorns:W/No.7407 of 1948) was pictured busy shunting whilst LONPOWER (Hawthorn Leslie:W/No.3792 of 1931) was spare. Despite LONPOWER being scrapped in 1966 and ERGON in 1968, steam remained in sole charge until the end of rail traffic in March 1981. This was due to the welcome arrival of a replacement steamer from Goldington Power Station in 1965 and another from Brimsdown Power Station in 1967.

A mile directly north of Acton Lane Generating Station was another generating station at Taylors Lane. It lay south west of Neasden Station on the ex-Great Central and Metropolitan Lines to the east of the North Circular Road. Rail connection was made to the Cross-London Line of the ex-Midland Railway from Cricklewood to Acton Wells Junction which bridged the Great Central and Metropolitan Lines to the north of the power station. With the attractions of Neasden Steam Shed and the London Transport depot in the vicinity in the sixties, it was not surprising that this location received little attention. On the 14th April 1962 NORTHMET (Robert Stephenson and Hawthorns:W/No.7056 of 1942) was in steam. This fireless had struggled with a solitary life here since delivery as a new locomotive. It was only in 1963 that company turned up in the shape of a battery electric locomotive from Luton Power Station. By 1970 the station was only operating at periods of peak load and the internal rail system was falling into disuse. Closure came in March 1972 and both locomotives departed for preservation in the following November.

Just across the county boundary from Hertfordshire, the rural Cambridgeshire village of Barrington shares coverings of wind swept cement dust with the works on its fringes. The plant was opened by the Eastwood Cement Company in 1926 and a narrow gauge system transported the chalk from the quarry to the crusher. A standard gauge branch known as the Barrington Light Railway, a mile and a half in length, connected the plant to the LNER Cambridge-Hitchin main line at Foxton. Modernisation in the early sixties included displacement of most of the narrow gauge quarry system by standard gauge to serve a new quarry and wagon tippler that was connected to the works sidings. The extension of the standard gauge network required additional locomotives and two Ruston and Hornsby diesel electrics were the first to be acquired. 7 (W/No.499435 of 1963) was still going strong working in the quarry on 19th January 1989 dwarfed by a Ruston Bucyrus diesel dragline loading overburden.

The track from the tippler split to serve two working faces.Usually two locomotives were busy in the quarry hauling rakes of seven or eight internal wagons. The site was taken over by Rugby Cement at the time of modernization and in the last years of operation the company had been generous to industrial railway enthusiasts in holding 'steam days'. These events have been particularly special as the steam took turns in working the commercial operations recreating the heady days of the past. Steam Sentinel No.7 (W/No.9376 of 1947) takes on a haul of chalk from the Ruston Bucyrus excavator on 3rd July 1996. However these quaint locomotives were no strangers at Barrington. Between 1965 and 1967 three steam Sentinels worked here. They had lost their original home when rail traction ceased at Totternhoe Works. Their eventual fate took an unusual turn when they were sold on to Thomas Hill of Kilnhurst. In his South Yorkshire shops major transformation would take place to convert them to diesel locomotives. Fortunately No.7 escaped this treatment and was on loan from the Rutland Railway Museum.

On the 23rd February 2005 the traffic manager for the railway had tears in his eyes. The closure of the quarry system was imminent and its passing was being mourned by a last 'steam day'. This was a landmark in industrial railway history as this was the very last cement works quarry railway to operate in the United Kingdom. The weather was suitably cold and raw with occasional snow flurries blowing in the wind. These hostile conditions on the site were offset by a company van dispensing free coffee. As usual two diesels were working into the quarry whilst the Avonside steamer DORA, on hire from the Rutland Railway Museum, aided and abetted the diesels with further loaded trips from the workings. In drab green, 4, a diesel hydraulic manufactured by Thomas Hill (W/No.186V of 1967) hauled loaded wagons to the tippler. The Barrington Light Railway remained and two diesels were retained for the dwindling coal traffic from Foxton. Line closure was now inevitable and these two locomotives departed for a scrapyard in Warwickshire in the Autumn of 2009. No.8, Thomas Hill diesel hydraulic and a loaded wagon are displayed at the works as a monument to this iconic industrial railway system.

In the sixties the low lying Lea Valley, from Brimsdown down to the mouth of the river into the Thames, was host to a string of gas works, power stations and factories. Until the boundary changes of 1965 Brimsdown Power Station was in the north east corner of Middlesex. Situated on the west bank of the River Lea, coal was delivered by barge. It was not until 1925 that the plant developed its own internal railway system which was accessed from the ex-Great Eastern Main Line from Cambridge to Liverpool Street just north of Brimsdown Railway Station. On the 16th June 1962 a bird's eye view was caught from the cooling towers of fireless ED1 SIR JAMES (Andrew Barclay:W/No.1550 of 1917) hard at work. ED2 LORD ASHFIELD was being charged (Andrew Barclay:W/No.1989 of 1930) and ED3 BIRKENHEAD (Robert Stephenson and Hawthorn:W/No.7386 of 1948), a conventional steamer, was looking neglected in a little shed. Rail traffic ceased in the closing months of 1971. After a stint at Fleetwood Power Station (and ED2 was later at Kearsley Power Station) both fireless made it into preservation. ED3 was called for further service at Acton Lane Generating Station before gaining preservation.

Three miles south of Brimsdown on the Cambridge to Liverpool Street Main Line is Angel Road Station. In the early sixties characters in duffle coats and gaberdine raincoats could be found lurking on Angel Road Bridge which carries the North Circular Road. The attraction was the dwindling BR steam worked traffic.This concrete structure overlooked the station on the north side with Tottenham Gas Works on the south side. The chain driven box like contraptions rattling round the yard of the gas works sounding like steam driven sowing machines were regarded with some indifference. That their attractive livery had some resemblance to the Crimson Lake of the Princess Coronations made no impact either. However on the 14th May 1960 both Sentinel steam locomotives were silent: 11 (W/No.9366 of 1945) and the ex-7 (W/No.9167 of 1935). Instead the Ruston and Hornsby diesel 12 (W/No.245033 of 1947) was doing the work. In December 1963 the elderly Sentinel was cremated 'in house' but 11 found refuge at Quainton Road in August, 1970. With the onset of North Sea natural gas production, coal gas manufacture was terminated at the works and rail traffic ceased early in 1972.

As the Cambridge to Liverpool Street Main Line continues south to the capital it is bridged by the Gospel Oak to Barking Line. The route eastwards to Barking crosses the River Lea to continue via Blackhorse Road and Walthamstow to reach Leyton Midland Road. This station was host to the adjacent scrap dealer of H. & J.R. Saunders based in the goods yard. If a steam locomotive can be described as 'distressed' then Samuel Williams No.1 was worthy of the description on the 11th October 1961 (Manning Wardle:W/No.1590 of 1903). Samuel Williams of Dagenham Dock was a favourite haunt of Industrial Railway Enthusiasts for its principal attraction was that most of the fleet comprised antique Manning Wardles. New diesels begun to be delivered in 1949 so steam gradually met an early demise here. No.1 arrived in Leyton in July 1961 to join a Peckett of 1941 build that had been in residence here since October 1956. The scrapping date for No.1 (and for the Peckett) is unknown but it would not be a surprise if the engine fell apart on the spot.

In the early sixties South West Essex stretched into the depths of London's environs until it reached the boundary of the River Lea. Consequently Bromley-By-Bow Gas Works which lay on the east side of the River Lea and Bow Creek was still in Essex. Founded by the Imperial Gas Company in 1870 this vast works was sited on land previously occupied by a rocket factory (the Congreve rocket of 1804 was developed here using propellant made at the nearby Royal Gunpowder Mills at Waltham Abbey.The rocket was first used in the Napoleonic wars). The venture failed as Imperial's 'Beckton' and in 1876 they were swallowed up by the Gas Light and Coke Company. A major disadvantage was that coal could only be delivered by barge. The works had to wait until 1912 before it was finally connected to a chord that ran from the London Tilbury and Southend Railway to the east of Bromley Station to the Great Eastern Railway line from Stratford to North Woolwich. On the 15th June 1960 traffic was slack. No less than four steamers were found on shed deprived of work. Only the youngest member of the fleet was in steam, a Peckett of the R4 class (No.2, W/No.2135 of 1953).

Traffic was light again on a further visit on the 15th July 1961. No.5, an Andrew Barclay, was in steam whilst the other four locomotives reclined in the shed. On the left hand road the black No.1 (Neilson:W/No.4397 of 1891) was looking the worse for wear and said to be ready for scrapping. It was similar in design to the Beckton Neilson side tankers with the added refinement of a weatherboard of doubtful protection. Next to No.1, Bromley's Peckett No.2 was under repair and at the end of the line No.3 (Robert Stephenson and Hawthorns:W/No.7309 of 1946) was looking as if repairs had been abandoned. On the right hand road and ready for work was the spare engine, the black No.4 (Andrew Barclay:W/No.1666 of 1920). In 1962 a Hibberd diesel arrived and worked alongside the steam. No.1 lingered on to 1963 when the steamer met its fate locally in a Canning Town scrapyard along with Nos.3 and 4. Nos. 2 and 5 followed in 1966. The Hibberd found a new home. Gas production ceased in 1970 but nostalgic enthusiasts can reminisce by catching sight of the remaining seven gasholders from a District Line train.

Only a mile further north and close to the eastern bank of the River Lea was Bow Generating Station. It was situated in the historic district of Old Ford, once the site of an ancient crossing when the river was wide with a fast current. The Great Eastern Railway offered a rail connection about a mile west of Stratford Station. On 30th April 1960, under the auspices of the Central Electricity Generating Board, MET (Hawthorn Leslie: W/No.2800 of 1909) was safeguarding its reputation for a smart appearance. MET arrived from Acton Lane Generating Station in Middlesex at the end of the 1940's. MET's name reflected one of the previous owners at Acton Lane, the abbreviation for the Metropolitan Electric Supply Company. In the shed on the same date dwelt 5 (Hawthorn Leslie:W/No.3653 of 1927) which hailed from Barking Generating Station at Creekmouth, a few miles down river. Rail traffic ceased in 1966. 5 was sold for scrap in 1968 whilst MET has lodged at various preservation sites before settling down at the Stratford and Broadway Railway Society.

Much of London's heavy industry grew on the banks of the River Thames. In the 1860's the Gas Light and Coke Company was searching for a site for a works to meet the increasing requirement for gas in the Capital. In 1868 they bought land of some 500 acres on the East Ham marshes at Gallions Reach near Barking Creek. In keeping with those who look for a name for themselves for posterity the property was called 'Beckton' in honour of Simon Beck a director, and later, head of the company. In November 1870 the first gas was produced at Beckton Gas Works. As the works continued to expand and diversify it became a major employer in South West Essex. Such a complex demanded an extensive internal railway layout and at its peak this amounted to 42 track miles. In its time the system boasted three sheds including a roundhouse built in 1875. On the 30th April 1960 No.4 (Andrew Barclay:W/No.1720 of 1921) was in poor shape outside the roundhouse. No.4 was scrapped in 1961. Its two brothers (No.36 and No.39) were scrapped in 1961 and 1960 respectively. The roundhouse was demolished in 1963.

If enthusiasts visiting the gas works were not satiated by its attractions then they could top up by migrating to next door. For to the west of the gas works lay the by-products works with a menu of tar, pitch, creosote and fertilizer manufacture to fill the lungs. The internal railway system was nominally independent from the gas works system and expressed its difference by a splendid livery of maroon. Like their neighbour the original mainstay at the by-products were steamers of Neilson build. Six new locomotives were delivered between 1892 and 1902 from Neilson and Neilson Read. On the 20th April 1963 No.1,No.2 and No.3 had survived. No.3 (Neilson:W/No.4571 of 1892) was photographed outside the shed having finished for the day. The maroon Neilsons were noticeably more brassy than their gas works brothers and were further embellished by their brass running numbers on the smokebox doors.

The loco shed on 20th April 1963 held a mixed bag of treasures. In the yard were two locomotives in varying shades of maroon and the other in sombre black. The snout of the by-products sole fireless can just be seen (No.12, Hawthorn Leslie:W/No.3595 of 1924) coupled to No.13, a Hawthorn Leslie (W/No.3308 of 1918). Attached to the Hawthorn Leslie was the black No.14 built by Peckett (W/No.2083 of 1947). No.14 was delivered new to the by-products but No.13 arrived from British Industrial Plastics of Oldbury in 1946, whilst the fireless had managed the short distance from Barking Generating Station at Creekmouth In the depths of the dimly lit shed was another Peckett (No.9) under repair whilst Neilsons No.1 and No.3 were both at work that day. Neilson No.2 was in the works for an overhaul. The green stranger in the camp was Neilson No.29 (W/No.5231 of 1897, rebuilt at Beckton in1930). The gas works locos rarely strayed from their home though No.29 had been transferred to the by-products in May of 1962.

The mainstay of the gas works was the Neilsons. Why the company chose Neilson of Glasgow is not clear although they were the principal locomotive builder of the nineteenth century. The Great Eastern Railway may have exerted some influence as they took the works traffic on to the main line hauled by locomotives also manufactured by Neilson. There were three types of squat design to enable them to work through the retort houses. In the sixties No.1 (built in 1870) was the only survivor of seven well tanks (at the rear of No.4 on page 18). This loco received much tender loving care. In 1959 the Mechanical Engineer was quoted as saying 'She'll last out her century at least and she'll be scrapped over my dead body!' This wish was only partially granted and No.1 passed to the Penrhyn Castle Museum in December 1963. Only No.25 of the five saddle tank 'Jumbos' made it into the sixties. The most numerous class were the side tankers. The class of ten was still complete in 1958. No.13 (W/No.2598 of 1880, rebuilt Beckton 1929) was pictured on the 20th April 1963 by which time only No.23 also remained.

Resembling a barn rather than a loco shed, this structure was built at about the time of nationalization of the gas industry. It was fitted with the luxury of illuminated pits although this offered cold comfort for the men as the winds whistled through the building from across the marshes. The single track into the shed fanned into seven roads akin to some tramway depots of past times. In this view on 20th April 1963, fireless No.34 (Robert Stephenson and Hawthorns:W/No.7665 of 1951) was under charge and not to be moved. The gas works had two fireless which operated in the purifying plant. Neilson No.13 (W/No.2598 of 1880, rebuilt Beckton 1929) was dead and accompanied by an intruder 'Planet' diesel No.46 (Hibberd:W/No.3910 of 1959). The third shed was a small rather dilapidated affair that usually stabled the two steamers for the overhead retort lines.

The change over to diesel traction brought over eighty years of steam into an unmitigated decline. In 1957 it was originally envisaged that 25 diesels would be required to replace 37 conventional steamers. In the event only eleven diesels came on stream due to the running down of railway operations. They were all of Hibberd manufacture and delivered between 1958 and 1961. Their compact size, absence of exposed running gear as well as the essential short wheelbase for the tight curves suited Beckton operations. Consequently by 1959 a slow but persistent steam slaughter set in at the works. Visitors would look askance at rusting steamers dumped on sidings waiting their fate. On 30th April 1960 No.30, stripped of identity, waits on death row by the sludge pit. No.30 (along with No.31) was a carbon copy of a Neilson side tanker built in Beckton's own workshops. The company claimed that this exercise was to give their apprentices valuable experience. Neilsons were not amused and threatened legal action.

The apple green and maroon liveries of the steam locomotives were a welcome splash of colour within a grim environment. The elaborate lining out would have suited many main line locomotives. The apple green was inherited by the diesels as well as the brass number plates although the 'No.' was dropped. Senior engineers maintained that although there were many things they would like to change at Beckton it was not going to be the locomotive livery. The external condition of the surviving steam engines at the gas works deteriorated in the sixties but the by-products continued a smart turn out for their locomotives. On the 28th June 1962 no less than six engines were in steam at the by-products whilst No.10 (Peckett:W/No.1575 of 1920) was out of use and was scrapped the following month. Towards the end of the sixties the gas works diesels had penetrated the by-products territory and only an out of use No.1 and fireless No.12 remained. The very last train to leave the Beckton complex on 1st June 1970 was carrying pitch from the by-products.

The steam colliers docked at two deep water piers where their cargo of coal was discharged into capacious hoppers. On 20th April 1963 No.7 (Bagnall:W/No.2657 of 1942) commanded a view of the cranes and the river.This work worn locomotive, driven by a gaffer whose face had been sculptured by the austere working conditions, would couple to sixteen hopper wagons laden with coal. No.7 would then ascend the steep grades to the high level lines that served the horizontal retort houses. Peckett No.2 and No.7 were working this duty, fitted with Westinghouse pumps to release the air operated bottom discharging doors of their wagons replenishing the internal bunkers in the retort houses. Coke was collected from the retorts via the low level lines. Although it was planned to eliminate steam, the diesels could not work into the horizontal retorts due to the restrictive clearances. Since the expected abandonment of these retorts had not taken place steam had the last laugh. Apart from the fireless, two engines were steamed daily. In June 1969 the last coke oven was discharged and one hundred years of the 'Bad Light and Smoke Company' came to an end.

If Beckton Gas Works was first choice for the industrial railway enthusiast in London then the Port of London Authority had to be second. However there was less time remaining to savour steam in the docks. The gas works company had built a two mile branch in 1871 joining the Great Eastern Railway from Stratford to North Woolwich at Custom House. Just to the west of the junction of these two lines, at the east end of the Royal Victoria Dock, was the engine shed of the Royal Docks system. On the 30th April 1960 no less than sixteen steamers sat on desolation row on a siding near the shed. This funereal line up was a mix of the two locomotive types that made up the roster in the last years. 79, 83, 86, 87, 88, 80 represented the 'austerities' whilst 62, 58, 60,77, 67, 51, 49, 59, 72 constituted the Hudswell Clarke side tankers. The exception was 69, a side tank of Hawthorn Leslie build. Dieselisation was swift and the annihilation of steam was completed in four years. Yet this new regime was also to suffer an early termination. The docks were already in decline in the early sixties which was accelerated by container traffic. Consequently the railway system was also contracting and in 1970 it closed completely.

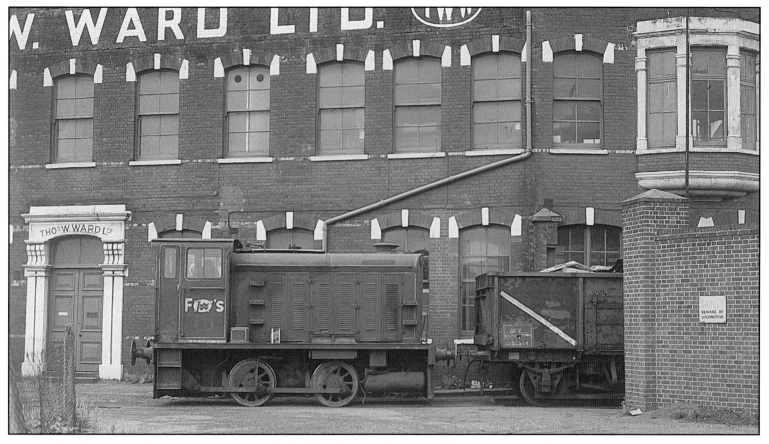

In 1850 the Victoria Dock Company constructed a dock to the east of Bow Creek. It was sited immediately north of the Stratford to North Woolwich line that had been completed in 1847. A swing bridge carried the railway across the eastern entrance of the dock. This was not good news due to the conflicting traffic requirements of rail and shipping. The solution was to build a diversion around the north side of the dock to join the original line just west of Silvertown Station. The abandoned line became known as the Silvertown Tramway. The resulting spur served the numerous pungent industries flourishing on the land between the line and the north bank of the Thames. By the time of a visit on 1st September 1981 the only remaining rail served facility was T.W. Ward's scrapyard near the junction with Silvertown Station. The Hudswell Clarke diesel (W/No.D1009 of 1956) propelling wagons though the gates of the scrapyard still wears the faded lined green of its previous life with Fry's in rural Keynsham. The diesel mechanical arrived at these more humble surroundings in August 1980. A John Fowler diesel, in faded maroon, was dumped at buffer stops on a siding outside the works and a Hibberd diesel (W/No.3900 of 1959) was under repair.

For the industrial railway enthusiast with a penchant for diesels , this location was a fascinating place for its varied history of acquired locomotives. No less than twelve diesels worked at this small yard between 1952 and 1992 representing six builders. The John Fowler diesel (W/No.4210076 of 1952) had been out of use since 1975 and the long wait on death row finally ended in March 1984. On another visit on 24th July 1986 to the grassy sidings, the John Fowler had been replaced at the buffer stops by two more decaying diesels. The dismal scene was compounded by the remains of the works building which had been demolished. The Hudswell had been repainted in Ward's yellow and behind rested Ruston and Hornsby (W/No.398611 of 1956). The Ruston 88DS originated from Leabrook Ironworks, Wednesbury and operated only for a few months before being consigned to an unexpected demise. The worker was a Hudswell Clarke of 1964 build (W/No.D1291) sitting in the oily scrapyard. There was little activity now as only one train per month plied to Temple Mills. The bulk of the tramway had already been converted into a footpath so with the cessation of rail traffic in 1991, the tramway was no more.

The bleak and dreary North Thames Marshes continue east from Beckton to Purfleet and West Thurrock. For the industrial railway enthusiast this hinterland was still paradise in the sixties. Clustered together on the margins of the river had grown a mix of industries where the visitor was spoilt for choice. Immaculate maroon fireless crept about at the margarine works of Van den Berghs and Jurgens. Purfleet Deep Water Wharf had a mixed stock of steam and diesel and for the diesel inclined there was William Cory, Esso and Shell. However the principal contenders for choice were the plants associated with the cement industries. Thurrock Chalk and Whiting was a 'must do' with a fleet of seven steam locomotives. On the 28th October 1961 COMET (Bagnall:W/No.2879 of 1948) was working as was P.H.B. (Hawthorn Leslie: W/No.3760 of 1932) sitting behind the Bagnall. The condition of the engines was to be applauded in an industry well known for its generous dusting of the environment. P.H.B. went to the breakers in March,1966 and COMET followed in September,1967.

The quarries and plants served by the company were situated on the western edge of Thurrock on the north side of London Road. The line ran south from the quarrying and works areas tunnelling under London Road and then rising to bridge the London, Tilbury and Southend Main Line where wagons were exchanged. A further half a mile across the West Thurrock Marshes brought the railway to the Thames Jetties. By the time the Second World War broke out, traffic was being handled for Lafarge Aluminous Cement, Thurrock Flint and Alpha Cement. In the fifties decline was apparent as dumper trucks replaced the tracks in the Alpha Cement quarry. The locomotive stock in the Autumn of 1961 boasted four Andrew Barclay, one Bagnall, one Hawthorn Leslie and one Peckett. On a visit on the 2nd September 1961 three locomotives were in steam although on the 14th and 28th October 1961 four steamers were at work. On the latter date the working THURWIT represented Peckett's R2 class (W/No.1734 of 1927) whilst GEORGE sitting behind was spare (Andrew Barclay:W/No..1281 of 1912). These two accompanied each other to the scrappie in March, 1966.

On the 28th October 1961 only one of the brace of four Barclays was in steam. PLANET (W/No.747 of 1894) squats outside the corrugated affair that masquerades as an engine shed. By September 1967 their last steam locomotive had departed to face the torch apart from their most venerable Barclay of 1891 build that survives at Quainton Road. Dieselisation arrived in 1966 in the form of three brand new Rolls Royce diesel hydraulics. Future decline was now inevitable and continued through the next two decades. The Alpha Works closed in the late sixties whilst Thurrock Flint followed in the early seventies. Subsequent changes eventually brought the diesel trio into the ownership of Lafarge where they operated the remnants of the internal railway and limited transshipment to the main line. Road haulage displaced the remainder of the system in the late eighties and the diesels found another cement environment at Dunbar in East Lothian. Lafarge still have a presence at West Thurrock. In 2008 new rail sidings were installed to serve the distribution depot which is fed by the Hope Valley Cement Works.

A gentle stroll to the east from Thurrock Chalk and Whiting along London Road brought the industrial railway enthusiast to another haven of working steam. However this was no charming pastoral walk as London Road passed underneath the road works for the approaches to the first Dartford Tunnel (opened 1963). On the other side was situated Tunnel Cement. Consequently their site was also placed to the west of Thurrock with their quarries and works on the north side of London Road. On the 14th October 1961 no less than nine steam locomotives were to be found here. However unlike their neighbours at Thurrock Chalk and Whiting, Tunnel Cement had dabbled with diesels since 1938 and three Ruston and Hornsby of various vintages were scattered around the system. Next door had a preponderance of Barclays whilst Tunnel favoured Peckett giving a majority of seven. Cleanliness did not match Thurrock Chalk and Whiting standards but THOR (Peckett:W/No.1689 of 1925) looked respectable enough for any god in lined out dark green.

There was something akin to a mirror image in the way Tunnel's railway system resembled the competition on the other side of the Dartford Tunnel construction site. Again, an industrial tramway from the works travelled southwards to the Thames. This time the handicap of London Road was met with a level crossing before continuing to bridge once more the London, Tilbury and Southend Main Line where a trailing connection accessed the eastbound track. Another half a mile lay ahead across the West Thurrock Marshes to the riverside jetties. Soon after leaving the main line bridge behind the tramway split. One section continued straight on carried by an embankment that terminated in a deep water wharf whilst a branch veered to the east to serve a jetty in shallower water. ANGLO-DANE (Peckett:W/No.1318 of 1913) was lingering in the works on the 14th October 1961. Both THOR and ANGLO-DANE were members of the maker's R2 class.

Tunnel's locomotives were somewhat better off for nurturing than Thurrock Chalk and Whiting although their 'al fresco' shed in the works complex must have offered cold comfort from the east wind in Winter. Here on the 14th October 1961 both POLAND (Peckett:W/No.1994 of 1940) and SOUTHERN (Hunslet:W/No.1688 of 1931) were in steam and taking a break. A shed also existed in the quarry where a steamer was in store as well as shops where another steam engine was found under repair. None of the seven steam on location that day escaped the terror of the torch. The last two departed for the end in March, 1968. The Ruston 'hangers on' were augmented by three new Rolls Royce diesel hydraulics between 1965 and 1967, two Yorkshire Engine refugees from the Port of London Authority in 1970 and 1971 and a second hand Ruston from Pitstone Cement. The works closed in April 1976 and was rapidly dismantled. Although the cement industry on this tract of land now only exists on a small scale, shadows of the past remain. These 'moonscapes' created by chalk extraction are the subject of transformation through new development.

In the early sixties there was still more to consume of this feast of steam operated industrial railways in Purfleet and Thurrock. About a mile and a half east along London Road and situated on the south side of the London, Tilbury and Southend Main Line was the Wouldham Works of British Portland Cement. The plant originated as the Lion Cement Company as long ago as 1874. It was purchased by Pearson and Sons in 1898 who constructed additional rotary and chamber kilns. Their original intention was the supply of cement for their contract to build Dover Harbour. The extended and modernized works was absorbed by the BPCM Group in 1912. On the 2nd September 1961 THOR (Andrew Barclay:W/No.1391 of 1915) was the only engine in steam. A belt installed earlier in the year to convey chalk from the quarry to the works had decimated the steam roster from ten to three.

It cannot be a surprise that the set up at Wouldham had similar features to that at Tunnel and Thurrock Chalk and Whiting. The quarries lay again to the north of London Road. The path of the industrial tramway that brought the excavated chalk to the works lay underneath the London Tilbury and Southend Main Line as well as the branch to Upminster. This time London Road benefited from a bridge over the line. However Wouldham Works, built on the West Thurrock Marshes, stretched to the banks of the Thames. As was to be expected there was a rail served jetty as well as a creek with rails on both sides that functioned as a wharf. Steam cranes discharged clay and coal from barges and colliers and kept a balance by loading cement. With the closure of the quarry system only one locomotive was required in steam whose duties included attending to the exchange sidings that connected to the westbound track of the main line. On the 14th October 1961 STANLEY (Peckett:W/ No.1314 of 1913) was acting as spare engine to THOR.

With the incline from the works to the quarry no longer resounding to the thunderous exhaust of steam traction, the three remaining locomotives settled down to their last years. The track to the quarry was soon lifted although the old signal still stood sentinel over the wasteland. The engine shed was to be found on the west side of the works in the vicinity of the chamber kilns. This substantial building offered superior accommodation that would be the envy of their neighbours at Tunnel and Thurrock Chalk and Whiting. Two roads entered the running bay and a third road served the fitting shop. With seven of the inmates now scrapped the shed had become more capacious so HILTON (Peckett:W/No. 633 of 1896) had plenty of room in which to rest on 14th October 1961. This veteran was ostensibly out of use but both STANLEY and HILTON later worked the one engine in steam duty before their lives were terminated. The old Peckett was scrapped on site in 1963 and the other two received their last call in 1965. Dieselisation was restricted to but one locomotive delivered new from Rolls Royce in 1965. When Wouldham Works closed down the diesel hydraulic found work in a similar environment at the Swanscombe Works in February 1978.

A trickle of enthusiasts would have visited Kidbrooke to gaze at the elegant Victorian lines of No.111 ALDWYTH 339 (Manning Wardle:W/ No.865 of 1882). The depot here was constructed for the Air Ministry. Opened in 1918 it was serviced by the ex-SECR Blackheath to Dartford line. However when visited on the 2nd October 1961 it was under the control of the Ministry of Works. Although ALDWYTH had some do-it-yourself treatment that did not enhance its lines, it was essentially a standard Manning Wardle contractors locomotive of the period. The steamer toiled on construction jobs until sold to the RAF circa 1920 acquainting itself with Kenley Airfield and then Hendon Aerodrome before arriving at Kidbrooke. Not to be outdone was a venerable member of the diesel era sitting in the shed shadows (No.140 Andrew Barclay:W/ No.321 of 1936). Rail traffic ceased in February 1967 whereupon ALDWYTH was rapidly parcelled up and sent off for preservation the following month. The Barclay was not destined to share the retirement benefits of ALDWYTH. The locomotive was dispatched to a Greenwich scrappie, also in 1967, and cut up circa 1972

Although cement works are to be found nationwide, the greatest concentration originally grew on the Kentish side of the Thames Estuary. Between Dartford and Gravesend and besides the Medway Estuary and its lower reaches, a honeycombe of chalk quarries developed. These are now mostly worked out and overgrown. The Kent Portland Cement Company was situated on the Thames foreshore about half a mile north east of Stone Crossing Halt where traffic was exchanged with the ex-S.E. & C.R. main line. There was a substantial jetty on the river. The internal rails from the works and jetty tunnelled southwards under the main line to reach the chalk pits. The cement industry was not slow to dieselise and Sentinel's efficient designs won favour. On 22nd July 1961 both of their 1959 built diesel hydraulics were at work. However the works must have been loath to lose its steamers as no less than three were still on site. Here is ARTHUR (Manning Wardle:W/No.1601 of 1903) which was conveniently acquired from P. & W. Anderson on completion of their contract in 1922. In 1967 the Peckett of 1940 and the Robert Stephenson and Hawthorns of 1947 passed to a Bexley Heath scrapyard but ARTHUR retired to pastoral surroundings on the Kent and East Sussex Railway. The works closed in 1970.

Further east, the Empire Paper Mills at Greenhithe were a close neighbour of the Kent Cement Works. Their *dampfheizerlokomotive*, as the Germans called them, was delivered from Orenstein and Koppel's works in Drewitz, near Potsdam in 1907 (A.Koppel:W/No.2499). Fireless locomotives were numerous on the Continent and a sprinkling can still be found in steam across Europe. Not so in this country where they found limited favour. The reason for a paper mill choosing fireless locomotives is obvious; in 1907 no locomotive manufacturer in this country had touched them and thus Empire turned to Germany. The foreigner was out of use on the 4th April 1964 but this homegrown Andrew Barclay fireless stable mate (W/No.1561 of 1917) was photographed in steam.

Despite the wisdom of operating fireless locomotives in a paper mill , Empire also had a conventional steam locomotive on the roster. If that was not enough, steam cranes worked amongst the bales. Their attractive Peckett (W/No.1880 of 1935) was also in steam on 4th April 1964. NELSON was a member of the maker's R4 class. The locomotive arrived from the Aylesford Paper Mills at New Hythe near Maidstone in February 1959. The Empire Mills were opened in 1908 and constructed within the historic grounds of Ingress Abbey. Like the Kent works, the mill also made connection with the North Kent Main Line. A steeply graded single track spur formed a junction with the down line just to the east of Greenhithe station. The rail system served a jetty on to the Thames which received imported pulp. NELSON was scrapped in 1970, closely followed by the two fireless in 1971 after the cessation of rail transport. When the mills were dismantled the site was redeveloped for housing although the abandoned and trackless pier still juts out into the river.

Swanscombe Cement Works again made connection with the ex-S.E. & C.R. North Kent Line via a steeply graded single line that descended from the exchange sidings at Craylands to the works. The works lay to the north of the main line from which a tramway extended for half a mile across Swanscombe Marshes to Bell Wharf on the Thames. Southwards from the works the single track 'main line' burrowed underneath both the North Kent Line and a minor road. It continued through old workings with two more short tunnels under lanes to terminate in a vast pit some one and a quarter miles from the works. On 22nd July 1961 No.6 (Hawthorn Leslie:W/No.3717 of 1929) threads its way through the cutting formed by the old excavations with a train of chalk from the working pit. Seven identical locomotives of this design formed the fleet here. The steam was replaced in 1971 by transfer of Sentinel diesels from Kent Works and Johnsons Works after closure. Rail traction ceased in 1982 when the usable chalk was exhausted.

The Northfleet Deep Water Wharf was situated on the Thames to the west of The Creek. It was opened in 1868 by the Northfleet Coal and Ballast Company for shipping chalk, whiting and ballast and for the delivery of coal. Their railway system served three local cement works and associated chalk quarries. A severe gradient ascended to Northfleet Station Sidings. When the Northfleet quarries were approaching exhaustion the company crossed the river to develop their interests in West Thurrock. Meanwhile the Northfleet quarries were worked out by 1920 and sold in 1921 when the company went into liquidation. Fortunes were revived by the Kent Deep Water Wharf Ltd which was later reincarnated as the Northfleet Deep Water Wharf Ltd. By the time of a visit on the 22nd July 1961 traffic was virtually restricted to the adjacent New Northfleet Paper Mills. BRADLEY (Peckett: W/No.1950 of 1938) sat outside the shed in steam waiting the call for work. Sheltering inside was NORTHFLEET (Peckett:W/No.2080 of 1946) and a Ruston and Hornsby diesel electric (W/No.412713 of 1957). BRADLEY was scrapped in 1965 and NORTHFLEET followed in 1967.

During the mid-1920's the majority of the works and quarry lines in North Kent were converted to standard gauge. Previously it had not occurred to the works owners to do such a thing as traditional water transport was available on the Thames and Medway. Internal systems had given rise to a myriad of gauges. Standard gauge conversion formed part of the reconstruction at Bevan's Works, Northfleet in 1926. A new line was built to connect the works and chalk quarries via a tunnel to the east of the original tunnel which had carried a narrow gauge line. The works was linked to the national network by former trackbeds to the Perry Street Siding of the ex-London, Chatham and Dover Railway Gravesend West Branch. On 2nd October 1961 the locomotive stud was a Peckett duo. The plateless 4 (W/No.829 of 1900) was enjoying a leisurely day whilst 5 (W/No.967 of 1902) reclined in the shed. Both locomotives spent previous lives at cement works in North Kent.

In this view the locomotive shed can be glimpsed to the left whilst No.4 sizzles in the yard. Two locomotive sheds were originally built, one adjacent to the works site and the other near the pumping plant. The latter pumped chalk slurry to the works, a later development that reduced railway operations. The cluttered yard was typical of the sixties and compares markedly with the more clinical neat and tidy yards of to-day. No less than three different species of internal user wagons reside in the yard. Rail traction ceased in September,1964 and was replaced by a conveyor installation. The steamers lay idle until scrapped in 1966. The Associated Portland Cement Maufacturers absorbed all the cement plants in North Kent (except Halling) between 1900 and 1949. In 1970 they opened a large modern works at Northfleet on the site of the existing Bevan's Works to centralize operations and thus close the older plants although a chalk operation at Swanscombe remained active.

A few years before the onset of the First World War the English locomotive manufacturers were beginning to wake up to the concept of fireless locomotives. Andrew Barclay took the lead in manufacture and their first successful design appeared in 1912. By 1961 they had produced 114 machines. Nine other English locomotive builders followed this trend and outshopped 49 examples. Clearly Andrew Barclay remained the market leader. Industrial Railway Enthusiasts in the sixties with a passion for fireless locomotives would have made for the Imperial Paper Mills at Gravesend. No less than four fireless were on display on the 22nd July 1961.Two of these were in steam and both originated from Andrew Barclay. IMPERIAL No.1 (W/No.2373 of 1956) was pictured in sombre lined black whilst IMPERIAL No.3 (W/No.1496 of 1917) sported lined green.

The other two residents were again exports from the Orenstein and Koppel works in Germany. IMPERIAL No.2 (W/No.5900 of 1912) was photographed out of use and MARION (W/No.4708 of 1911) in green with red frames was stored in a warehouse surrounded by paper rolls. Bells were usually fitted as whistles would consume valuable steam. The mill was founded in 1912 on a riverside site to the west of the former Gravesend West Station. A network of sidings developed in the vicinity that served the mill as well as cement and whiting works. The Gravesend West Branch closed to freight in 1968. The first locomotive to face the cutters was IMPERIAL No.2 in Rochester in September 1968. MARION met her end at Creekmoor in early 1969 and IMPERIAL No.3 was scrapped on site in the Spring of 1979. However IMPERIAL No.1 was spared the slaughter to enter the hallowed halls of the National Railway Museum in July 1978 and now rests in spotless condition at Shildon. The mills site was redeveloped in the mid-1980's as the Imperial Business Estate.

In the latter part of the nineteenth century there were seven cement works packed into less than half a mile of the eastern shore of Limehouse Reach on the River Medway. This area of chalk hills and salty mud flats forms a peninsular bounded on both sides by a meander of the river. These works suffered a turbulent history of disputes over rights to the chalk. Beaver closed in 1900, Bridge and Globe in 1901 and Quarry, Beehive and Phoenix in 1907. The remaining works, Crown, was eventually modernized and became the Crown and Quarry works by absorbing the sites at Beehive, Beaver and Quarry. In 1954 the last quarry to be worked was opened. Transhipment took place with the ex-Southern Railway at Strood Wharf. In December 1962 chalk quarrying ceased and the works closed for manufacture in 1963. On the 4th March 1961, C.F.S. (Robert Stephenson and Hawthorns: W/No.7742 of 1952) was propelling wooden bodied tipper wagons to the quarry for loading through a surreal chalky landscape. J.G.B., an Avonside of 1921, was languishing in the shed waiting for repairs that never transpired and was scrapped in 1964. SOUTHFLEET, a Peckett of 1928, was the spare engine. Both working locomotives moved on to operate in new chalky environments in Oxfordshire and Essex.

Downstream from Limehouse Reach, as the Medway thinned into wandering meanders, was Holborough Cement Works. This Lower Medway site was some five miles from the environs of Rochester and squeezed between the ex -S.E. & C.R. line from Strood to Maidstone and the A228 road. Two connections were afforded to the main line. The southern connection was laid when the works was built in the mid-1920's and descended an incline to cope with the difference in levels. The north connection was adapted from a war time siding. On the 28th May 1960 a mixed bag of locomotives were found at the works. Lovers of the antiquated would have been delighted with the Aveling and Porter (W/ No.9449 of 1926). This machine was to be the last of the line from the Rochester based firm. By 1926 the design was well past its prime as evidenced by the seven years that had elapsed since Aveling and Porter had built a similar 'traction engine on rails'. Although relegated to spare it had been in steam the previous month. Behind the Aveling and Porter was FELSPAR (Manning Wardle:W/No.1846 of 1914) in steam on mundane stationary duties rather than active service. HORNPIPE (Peckett:W/No.1756 of 1928) was at work in the yards.

The two quarries that serviced the works, both chalk and clay, lay to the west of Holborough Village. Both operated three foot gauge systems. Crossing the A228 was avoided by pumping the chalk as a slurry and the clay was delivered via an aerial ropeway. The chalk quarry system was converted to standard gauge in 1954 although, like Houghton Regis, the layout remained unconnected to the works system. Consequently the standard gauge roster increased. On 28th May 1960 LONGFIELD (Peckett W/No.1747 of 1928) was in 'as received' condition when drafted in from Johnson's Works, Greenhithe, earlier in 1960, to work in the pits. Its neglected appearance was the result of its redundancy due to dieselisation at Greenhithe. Johnson's had conducted some surgery on chimney and cab for tunnel clearance. The do-it-yourself style would not have impressed Peckett but this was to be redeemed later by reinstatement of suitable body parts from the maker. Another legacy from Greenhithe was the dumb buffers which LONGFIELD was allowed to keep. In the quarry shed TUMULUS (Robert Stephenson and Hawthorn W/No.7813 of 1954) was under repair whilst Holborough's sole Sentinel diesel was at work in the pits. Most rail traffic had finished by 1971 and production was wound up in 1984.

The busy County of Kent would not appear to afford the visitor areas of remoteness although the Hundred of Hoo peninsular has this quality. The flat featureless landscape surrounded by marshland once carried a passenger service to Grain and Allhallows-on-Sea from Gravesend but the lack of custom brought closure in December,1961. However the line to Grain remained open to serve freight traffic. Berry Wiggins opened the first oil refinery on the peninsular at Kingsnorth in 1932 connecting to the Southern Railway branch line via a spur near Hoo Junction. The site was host to an ancient petrol locomotive and a solitary steam locomotive on April 4th !964. Two Motor Rail locomotives were recorded as derelict here in 1946 as No.1 (W/No.4204 of 1929) and No.2 (W/No.4217 of 1931). During the visit it was said that No.1 had incorporated parts from No.2 and was now resurrected as spare engine. No.2 was scrapped. Subsequent years brought two Drewry Car/Vulcan Foundry diesel locomotives to rescue the strange pair. Rail traffic ceased in early 1972 and the refinery was defunct by 1977. However the physical connection with the Grain branch was not removed until 2002.

During this 1960s many 'gems' survived to be hunted down across the land. The solitary steamer at Berry Wiggins, for instance, was doubly prized. Not only was it the product of a builder who turned out very few steam locomotives (Brush W/No.314 of 1906) but it had also fallen into the hands of the Great Western. Powlesland and Mason were contracted to shunt the Swansea Harbour Trust lines and the Brush was their No.6. When the GWR acquired the port they later absorbed the nine Powlesland and Mason locomotives in 1924 including No.6. They were not seen as a long term proposition but No.6 underwent some 'Swindonisation' and became 921. Sugar Beet and Crop Dryers Limited of Eynsham bought 921 in 1928 and then sold the engine on to Berry Wiggins in 1931 who converted the ex-921 to oil burning. When visited on April 4th 1964 the embellished engine was in steam and looking good. It was to cease work in the same year before passing into preservation in 1968.

Across the Medway from the Hundred of Hoo peninsular lies the Isle of Sheppey. Its low lying marshy scenery has little to commend it despite attracting caravan sites and holiday camps. If holidaying delights were to be found on Sheppey, the heavy industry spawned by the Isle would not be included. In the 1930's the industrial skyline of Queenborough gave vent to the unwelcome fumes of glue, chemical and glass works as well as a steel rolling mill. To-day this industrial legacy is represented by the rolling mills which still survive at Queenborough (as well as the steel works at Sheerness). The weather was hot and close when the steel mill was visited on August 21 1991. A mixed bag of six diesels were found on the railway system serving this installation. Here ELEMENTARY (English Electric:W/No.D1229 of 1967) shunts a flat wagon in the shed area whilst the forlorn 16, still in its fading ex-Army colours, awaits the unknown (Vulcan Foundry:W/No.5259 of 1945/Drewry Car:W/No.2176 of 1945). In November 1994, 16 was to enjoy an improved scenic environment on the Lavender Line at Isfield in Sussex. ELEMENTARY was not so fortunate and was cut up on site in 2003.

Four separate branch lines originally connected the Sittingbourne to Sheerness Branch of the Southern Railway to Queenborough wharves, piers and industries. The only remaining branch now serves the rolling mill and continues down to a pier at Hope Reach alongside The Swale. The wharf was built for coal shipments in 1896 but in more recent years has seen ship breaking and exported rolled steel. Nowadays Istil (UK) Ltd. imports billets to produce bars and rods at the mill. There are very few industrial rail systems left that are redolent of the sixties but the Queenborough set up must be one of them. The delights include the ramshackle two road shed that once existed for Settle Speakman to service the local works with their locomotives as well as the unprotected crossing over Rushenden Road. The rickety track meanders around Hope Reach within sight of beached Thames Barges to terminate at the pier. A penchant for ex-Army locomotives continues with a stock of four Andrew Barclay diesels repatriated from the British Army of the Rhine. On 6 April 2006 a battered 873 (Andrew Barclay: W/No.512 of 1966) skirts the shallows propelling empties from the mill to the pier.

Back on the mainland on the other side of The Swale in countryside as dismal and flat as that of Sheppey there still operates the quintessence of industrial narrow gauge railways. Lloyd's had begun to make use of steam locomotives on their rails around Sittingbourne Mill and Milton Creek Wharf in 1905 replacing the horse drawn tramways. The creek was prone to silting up although china clay was still being unloaded by barge in the 1960's. The company overcame this problem by constructing a new dock at Ridham to take advantage of the deeper waters of the Swale Estuary. Consequently the railway was extended for three and a half miles to Ridham in 1913. Further traffic was generated by the opening of a new mill at Kemsley about half way along the route in 1924. A gradual transition to road transport in the 1960's brought closure in October 1969. With foresight Bowaters Lloyd sought to preserve the line and a two mile stretch from Sittingbourne to Kemsley is now a living museum of essentially the original stock and locomotives. On 15th November 2008, MELIOR (Kerr Stuart:W/No.4219 of 1924) and TRIUMPH (Bagnall:W/No.2511 of 1934) take a break outside their reconstructed shed at Kemsley Down.

About one mile due south of Sittingbourne was the singularly rare operation of APCM's Highsted chalk pits. It was rare on two counts. The standard gauge system was isolated with no connection to the main line network being used internally to transport chalk to their washery. In addition the track was electrified using third rail which would have given to-days health and safety a nightmare. This quaint system was home to three identical electric locomotives. Two of these were fitted with Metrovick equipment and the other by GEC. The latter was built by Hawthorn Leslie although it's possible that this builder manufactured all three. All this kit came from G. and T. Earle's Hope Works in Derbyshire in 1953. Highsted's only steamer spent its last days here and on the 23rd April 1962 the disintegrating frames, wheels and cab were the last remnants of TAY, an Andrew Barclay. On the same date the electric locomotive photographed was formerly No.2 (built Metrovic 1929) but a repaint had removed its identity. The works closed in 1970.

Sittingbourne was host to another unusual system located a mile and a half to the east of the town. This internal railway served the clay pits near Little Murston from just north of the Smead Dean Cement Works on the east bank of Milton Creek. The distance of one and a quarter miles was opened in 1933 and laid to the exceptional gauge of four feet and three inches. A historical explanation for this choice has not yet surfaced although it has been suggested that a 'train set' of two steam locomotives and tipper wagons were on sale at the time and suited the job. The steamers were eventually scrapped (in 1949 and 1962) and replaced by a Planet diesel locomotive (W/No.3373 of 1949) which was delivered new. The 'hub' of the system was at East Hall and known as Sittingbourne Works. On a quiet day on the 23rd April 1962 there was time to examine the primitive tipper wagons here and the strewn debris characteristic of the period. The rear of the diesel could just be seen lurking in the dark recesses of the shed.

To the east of Sittingbourne lies the Kent Coalfield. The Garden of England gives cover to coal measures which are completely concealed by thick layers of younger rock strata. In the 1960's four pits remained in production forming the South Eastern Division of the NCB. Snowdown Colliery at Nonington was sunk during the mid-twenties and began winding coal in 1927. Although established as Snowdown Collieries Ltd., the company had merged with Pearson and Dorman Long Ltd. on opening in 1927. Three new locomotives were ordered from Avonside and delivered to Snowdown. The trio were destined to spend all of their commercial life in the Kent Coalfield. However ST.MARTIN (W/No.2064 of 1931) was a casualty before mining expired at Snowdown. On the 23rd August 1973 the Avonside was the worse for wear with all plates removed in preparation for the end. Andrew Barclay diesel mechanical (W/No.382 0f 1951) provided company. By the end of the year both were in the hands of a Rochester Scrappie.

On the 23rd August 1973, ST.DUNSTAN (Avonside:W/No.2004 of 1927) and an 'austerity' built by Hunslet (W/No.3825 of 1954) were enjoying a foray in the pit yard. The 'austerity' had managed a transfer from Betteshanger Colliery at the tail end of 1972. In black with yellow lining and lettered South Eastern Division No.9, the Hunslet contrasted with the lined Cambridge Blue of the Avonside. On a subsequent visit in the Autumn of 1976 the halcyon days for the steamers appeared to be drawing to a close. Already on site were ex-British Railways diesel electrics 12131 and 15224 ready to oust them. The pair had been sold off to the Kentish Colliery of Betteshanger before migrating to Snowdown in mid-Summer 1976. However they were still not yet serviceable and were waiting for batteries that Ashford Works were unable to supply. 15224 eventually became the pit's operational locomotive but steam still struggled on for a few years as the diesel-electric was troublesome.

On the 29th March 1983 Snowdown yard was run down and desolate. Coal had not been sent by rail since 1978 and dumpers took over all the internal rail traffic in 1979. Consequently NCB 8, the Thomas Hill/Sentinel (W/No.120c of 1962) diesel hydraulic, dispatched from Birch Coppice Colliery in December 1979, had seen little use. The British Railways connection had been severed and the drunken poles in the exchange sidings were the legacy to overhead wires that once served the dual equipped E5000 series electric locomotives. There was still occasional movement when changing the ropes at the pithead which was handled by John Fowler diesel (W/No.4160002 of 1952) which had been in residence since 1958. On this last visit the faded and weatherbeaten John Fowler was dumped in the yard. ST.DUNSTAN stood guard outside the substantial shed repainted in all over blue. Inside languished the other Avonside ST.THOMAS (W/No.1971 of 1927) and the yellow NCB 8. It was to be another two years before the moribund steamers received the good news to accompany the John Fowler for preservation in April 1985. NCB 8 waited another two years in solitude before departing for preservation.

Croydon Gas Works in Surrey formed part of a 'triple whammy' for industrial railway enthusiasts. The works was situated on the south side of the ex-L.B.& S. C.R. branch from West Croydon at Waddon Marsh. The connecting sidings served the gas works as well as its neighbour, Croydon 'B' Power Station. On the north side of the line was yet another installation, the older Croydon 'A' Power Station. All three plants had their own allocation of internal locomotives. Enthusiasts were well served for visits by Waddon Marsh Halt, a characteristic Southern Railway concrete affair, on the doorstep of the awaiting attractions. On 15th June 1960 the grassy tracks at the gas works belied the fact that MOSS BAY (Kerr Stuart:W/No.4167 of 1920) was in steam. The locomotive was delivered new and was to serve this location until the end of steam. The name originates from the Moss Bay Steel Works at Workington where the mainstay of their fleet was of this type. JOYCE (Sentinel:W/No.7109 of 1927) was a member of a small class of four cylinder Sentinels. The unusual outline would be familiar to main line steam fans from the three examples delivered to the S.& D.J.R., 47190 surviving at Radstock until 1961. The roster at the works was completed by a chunky Avonside hiding behind JOYCE

On the 27th March 1961 two locomotives with colourful histories were found laid aside at British Industrial Sand at Holmethorpe in Surrey. Sentinel must be legendary for the variety of body shapes they created for their vertical boilered steam locomotives. The unique GERVASE (W/No.6807 of 1928) was an eccentric looking form of the genre. It began life as a conventional steam locomotive (Manning Wardle:W/No.1472 of 1900) before undergoing major surgery at the hands of Sentinel. At the rear of this machine was No.2 DOM although this appellation had been lost.This time the origins were with Sentinel as a steam railcar built for the Jersey Eastern Railway (W/No.6994 of 1927). When the Channel Island Railway closed the coach body was removed and the locomotive portion moved on elsewhere for further action. Acquired by British Industrial Sand in 1946 it was transformed in later years with a do-it-yourself sheet metal body. Looking akin to an armoured refugee from The Great War even Sentinel would have disapproved. Both passed to the Kent and East Sussex Railway in June of the following year. However DOM failed to survive preservation and was scrapped at Tenterden. GERVASE can still be inspected there albeit in unrestored condition.

Two main lines cross the North Downs from East Croydon to reach Redhill. Between Merstham and Redhill Stations a steeply graded branch descended via a tight curve from the ex-SER main line to British Industrial Sand. Here the single track expanded into the exchange sidings with an adjacent locomotive shed. At the eastern end of this layout single track resumed to pass under the ex-LBSCR 'Quarry Line' to access the processing plant. Twenty two years later on a very wet 29th March 1983 two diesels were stabled outside the shed; 1(Robert Stephenson and Hawthorns:W/No. 7901 0f 1958) and 3 (Andrew Barclay:W/No.332 of 1938). Inside the shed dwelt 2 (Baguley/Drewry Car: 2159 of 1941). The Robert Stephenson and Hawthorns locomotive was a 'Husky'. The makers had high hopes of this simple and robust design but sales proved poor. The excellent all round visibility was a feature that was not demonstrated by other industrial locomotive builders of the period. Sixteen 'Husky' were built of which three are extant in this country in preservation including 7901. Rail traffic ceased at Holmethorpe in April, 1990.

The majority of industrial railway systems in Hampshire were to be found around the coastal areas. The BP Oil fuels storage and distribution terminal at Hamble-le-Rice continues to function on the east side of Southampton Water. This installation is still connected to Hamble Station on the Portsmouth to Southampton line by a disused overgrown branch of one and a half miles. This short line was built towards the end of World War 1 so aircraft could be transported from Manchester to Hamble. The war ended before the line was operational and it was subsequently purchased for the carriage of oil. On 3rd October 1981 the well kept locomotives that worked the traffic were on view. The veteran Hudswell Clarke No.21 was built in 1950 (W/No.D707) and the Hunslet No.24 in 1967 (W/No.6950). By August 1985 a BR 08 had been working instead of No.24 from the exchange sidings to the depot. The line was last used in 1986 to bring crude oil from Wytch Farm in Dorset. This job was replaced by a pipe line and rail traffic ceased. No.21 was a prime candidate for preservation and was saved by the Mid-Hants Railway in November 1984 . No.24 moved on to a second life with BP in April 1989 at the Bitumen Oil Terminal on the Isle of Grain. BP still maintain an option for possible future use of the railway.